George & Janine

True-life Love Stories by

ELIZABETH BATTAGLIA

Part One of Two

www.georgeandjanine.com
Visit: George & Janine on Facebook

Published by Words In The Works LLC
info@wordsintheworks.com

Author's note

This story begins in 2015, when my 89-year-old mother asked if my sister and I would take her back to visit St. Tropez one last time. This wonderful trip prompted some storytelling and revelations that we had never heard before. We both agreed that we had not seen my mother so happy for a long time.

When we returned to England, we had further conversations about the past, and I wrote it all down. My intention was to create a book of her memoirs to give to my own children. This family history was recorded and given to them as Christmas gifts that same year. Of all the stories Mum shared, the story of how she met George Rogers, the handsome English soldier who stole her heart, was the favorite.

My mother died last November. I'll be forever grateful that my sister and I took this last journey with her. It left her at peace. This story is inspired by the events that led them to fall in love during the euphoric days leading up to the end of World War II.

Introduction

It is late summer, 1944. St. Tropez in the South of France. The German and Italian occupation of the town is finally over. French, American, and British troops are now in control, but it will be a long time before life in this once sleepy fishing village returns to any kind of normality. Buildings have been destroyed by German bombing in the final days before their retreat. Lives have been shattered. Food is scarce and there is little money to buy what food there is. Stories of atrocities and misconduct abound.

But freedom rules.

British troops are aboard ships making their way along the coastline stopping in at these devastated towns for "mopping up" operations.

Aboard one of these ships is George Rogers. A young private from London's East End who is serving in the Air Sea Rescue division.

On a sunny afternoon, he has a few hours leave and heads to the local beach. Fate brings him briefly into the life of the beautiful Janine Juppet, a young woman with heartbreaking war stories of her own.

There is an immediate rapport but there is also an expiration date on any connection they might have. George must leave in ten days, never to return. But what happens during those ten days changes their lives in ways they could never have imagined.

The sea sparkled in the late afternoon light. The setting sun hugged the horizon in a golden embrace. Mediterranean villas with their white-stucco walls and red ochre roofs rose up from the beach in a cozy semicircle. Palm trees swayed in the gentle breeze.

The young British soldier saw none of it.

His mind had drifted.

To the day before.

To this very spot on the beach.

And over and over, to the girl.

George had felt an instant attraction to her.

She was beautiful, but somehow reserved. She lit up with laughter, but in the next moment, seemed as if she was recalling a painful memory.

He could tell she wanted to appear carefree and yet the tears were always near the surface.

George wondered just what this young French girl had been through during these past four years. What had happened during the occupation of her country by the Germans and Italians?

His soldierly protective instincts wanted to assure her that whatever it was, it would never happen again—ever.

He had tried asking questions by stringing together the few French words he had picked up in Corsica a week earlier.

She would exchange glances with her two friends and with the smallest shake of her short brown curls, silence the other girls and change the subject. She always turned the conversation back to George. In her broken English, she tried asking him questions about *his* life. *His* war.

His vision of her now was crystal clear:

Propped up on her elbows. Beautiful, tanned legs stretched out on the white sand.

* * *

"George! For God's sake! We gotta go. We're due back on board in twenty minutes."

"It's almost 1800 hours, George. Are you comin' or not?"

George looked over to where his two friends had stood up and were dusting sand off their legs, both calling to him at once.

"Okay! Okay! I'm coming. Let's go."

George got up slowly and gave a last, long look around the beach. It was stupid to think that the girl would really show up.

The three friends started back up the narrow path that led away from the beach and back to the town. George lagged behind, kicking out despondently at random pebbles.

Yes, he had been stupid to think she would come but, jeez, that girl had been gorgeous. And her broken English! So very sexy.

George and his two friends, Colin and Basil, had gone to the beach in St. Tropez the day before in search of one thing:

French beauties in their sexy bathing suits.

The three soldiers were only stationed in this town for ten days and if the local scenery included French beauties, well…they wanted to make the most of it.

The girls on the beach they had seen so far really *were* beautiful—especially the three they'd chosen to sit near.

The one that he really fancied reminded him of a French cinema actress that he had seen on posters on their way along the French coast—he could even remember the name on the posters—Danielle Darrieux.

Green eyes with beautiful curved eyebrows and a smile that was open, friendly and yet alluring.

Maybe she might notice him. You never know—stranger things had happened!

George had taken a short stroll along the beach hoping the girls might join him. No luck! They stayed where they were.

Maybe he could impress her with his swimming abilities? He had his dad to thank for insisting that he learn to swim at the local pool in Hoxton during his teen

Plage des Graniers, 1944. George is at right.

years. Dad had been in the Merchant Marines in the first World War. He told harrowing stories about soldiers whose ships had sunk during battle and had drowned while waiting to be picked up. His dad had also insisted he and his brother, Jim, take boxing lessons. That had come in useful during his time in the service, too. George was tall, athletic and getting girls had always been easy.

George plunged into the water without hesitation and showed off with a few smoothly executed strokes.

He came out of the water, walked casually back to where his friends were sitting, sat down on his towel, and wondered what to try next.

The girl he had his eye on had started giggling uncontrollably while he was drying his toes and getting the sand off.

Hey, what was so funny? He wasn't going to put on his socks and shoes with sand still between his toes.

Basil, his so-called friend, had turned around and winked at the laughing girl and made a 'Yes, he's a bit mental' sign and pointed at George.

But the girl had suddenly stopped laughing and shook her head.

Then she gave George an amazing smile. Whoa! He pulled his towel a little closer to her, introduced himself, and she told him her name.

George. And Janine. They spent the next ten minutes trying to communicate. George valiantly used some of the French words he'd picked up. Janine giggled and replied in very broken English.

She was refined, so different from the girls he was used to dating. From the sidelong looks she gave him, maybe she fancied him too?

Her friends, Michelle and Mifi, seemed to have a better grasp of English and kept up the conversation easily. When Mifi introduced herself, Colin laughed trying to pronounce her name.

"What's that? MeeFee? Meeeee...Feeeee!" said Colin,

deliberately exaggerating the pronunciation. "Never heard of it."

Mifi joined in with the laughter and didn't seem to care he was having fun with her.

After hiking with the Girl Scouts, Mifi, Michelle, and Janine would swim at Plage des Graniers

George was glad when the others went for a short walk along the beach and he had Janine to himself. He wanted to know more about her.

"Do you live in St. Tropez, Janine?" He tried to say her name in the sexy French way she had told him how to pronounce it.

"Oui, yes! I live in a villa twenty minutes from this beach. We are able to come here now that the Italians have gone. Before that, we were not allowed at all."

Suddenly, a sad downward glance changed her demeanor and it made him want to hug her protectively.

"That is all over now," he said reassuringly. "You will be safe. There will never be another war."

George was confident that was true and anyway, it made Janine smile.

Suddenly Colin and Mifi were running towards them. George heard Colin shout that it was past time to leave.

"Do you come to this beach every day?" George asked urgently.

"Every day?" she shook her head slightly. "On the days my mother say I can come. But Mifi, she come every day."

It was his turn to shake his head.

'No, *you*, Janine."

He started pointing to his watch purposefully.

"Err, tomorrow...err...domani..." he tried.

Janine nodded her head. "Oui, d'accord. Demain—to-mo-row," she replied slowly.

"Four o'clock, we meet here. Like today? Quatro...? George asked.

"Oui, Oui! Quatre heures. I will see you."

She gave him that smile again.

"Here, we'll be here, waiting for you and your friends!" George pointed to where they were sitting.

"Oui, Yes. Ici, here, *Les Graniers,* a quatre heures," Janine giggled and then looked over at her friends. Her accent was the sexiest thing he'd ever heard. George gave her his big smile, a quick salute, and ran after his mates.

*Janine Juppet—George thought she looked like the
French film star, Danielle Darrieux*

Now George was wondering why Janine hadn't turn up today as arranged. The shaded, palm-tree lined path leading back to town seemed much shorter than when they had arrived and George walked along it slowly, not wanting to leave the beach. Colin and Basil were talking and sharing jokes up ahead, but he didn't feel like joining in. He'd been thinking about meeting Janine again since arriving and he couldn't accept that yesterday's brief encounter was nothing more than that: a brief encounter.

It might sound boastful, but he couldn't think of a time he'd been stood up before. And that was the difference, wasn't it?

The girls he knew from Shoreditch always showed up—they loved a good time.

Janine had been brought up differently. She looked like a film star and here she was, living in the South of France.

Last night, George had privately fantasized about playing the big hero, coming to Janine's rescue in a town that had been occupied by the enemy for the last four years and then bombed out of all recognition just a few weeks ago.

That fantasy quickly faded.

She hadn't shown and he would never see her again. George ran to catch up to Colin and Basil. They slapped him on the back and did their best to reassure him.

"Don't worry, George. We'll all go out tonight—there'll be other girls."

"Come on, mate. Forget about her. I know she was a looker but—"

Colin and Basil stopped the commiserations in mid-sentence when they suddenly heard loud girlish laughter. Janine and her two friends appeared around the corner. They seemed to be strolling along without a care in the world. George was so elated he didn't feel slighted or annoyed—just really happy to see her. He stood to attention and gave her a mock salute.

"Bonjour, Janine. Comment allez-vous?" He had practiced that phrase again and again lying in his bunk the night before. He'd also practiced a lot of other things he wanted to say to her, but they all went right out of his head. God, what the heck, why was he so nervous?

The three girls stopped talking and Janine's friends gave her a knowing smile. Janine reddened slightly.

"Bonjour, Georges, ca va bien, merci. I am good. You are going?"

"No, no, *they're* going. I'm staying now!" he replied brightly. He whispered to Colin and Basil, asking them to make up an excuse for why he would be late on board...broken ankle maybe? They shook their heads–*George! George! George!* But then they laughed and agreed they'd think of something.

George turned around and started walking back down the path with Janine. He could only think that this was meant to be—one more minute and they would never have seen each other again. Was this what people meant by fate?

George and Janine put their towels down next to each other and looked out over the glittering Mediterranean Sea. George opened his knapsack and took out the little English/French dictionary he had borrowed from someone on the ship the previous night. He glanced over at Janine.

"We've been here since four o'clock," he said in hesitant French. "I thought you weren't coming, we were leaving to—"

Janine quickly grabbed the dictionary. "I am very, very sorry. My friends would not be fast."

"Oh, God, no!" George broke in. "Please, don't misunderstand. I would have waited all night! I was just explaining we had to leave to get back on board our ship in time or get in trouble." George grinned at her. "But I don't care about getting in trouble now you're here. I'm happy you got here before I left."

Janine turned and gave him that smile. He had been calling it *The Film Star* smile when he thought about her.

He didn't think she realized how it lit up her face.

There was a long silence. Janine turned her head and glanced over at her friends who were getting ready to go for a swim.

George couldn't take his eyes off her, that beautiful profile. He had to stop staring! She'd probably think he was weird and obsessed. Janine got up and pulled off the dress that covered her bathing suit.

"We go to swim?" she asked.

George hurriedly started taking off his uniform and then remembered that Basil had told him there was a rip in the back of his swimming trunks.

Was that why they were laughing when he had come out of the water yesterday?

If she saw that tear again, she might feel he really *wasn't* good enough for her!

He tried to stand where the girls couldn't see the offending rip and motioned for them to walk in first.

The water at least was perfect—warm and welcoming.

The Mediterranean Sea, and the towns they had stopped at along the coast, were a world he had never even imagined growing up in the East End of London.

George had lived in London all his life and hadn't seen anything but the River Thames before joining the Air Sea Rescue.

He was only fifteen when the war had broken out in 1939. He had to enlist when he was eighteen and wasn't happy about it.

George didn't want to fight.

What did fighting ever prove?

George and Jim had once been the only two contenders left in a boxing tournament and George had been happy to lose to his brother.

What's more, when the call-up papers came, he was in the middle of taking classes to be an accountant while still working the full-time job he'd had since leaving school at fourteen. George had always worked hard and made his parents proud. His older siblings, Jim and Sylvia, also helped the family by working hard at their full-time jobs.

But George did go to fight and now the war was finally at an end. The Air Sea Rescue were travelling along the southern coast of France helping to 'mop up' as they put it. He had seen some exotic ports on his trip around the Mediterranean, and had met some interesting ladies, but he had always looked ahead for the next day and the next lady. Until now.

The crew of Air Sea Rescue vessel No. 2597.
George is in the back row, second from right.

When they came out of the water, they all sat down together and started to talk. They managed to exchange information about themselves, with lots of help from the little English/French dictionary.

"Where do you live, George?" Michelle asked.

"I'm a Londoner. Never stepped foot outside London before joining up in '42. I had to wait until then because I was only fifteen when the war started."

"You are twenty years old, now?" Janine questioned.

"Yep, twenty last March."

It made him feel like an adult to tell them that. He was sure they must be younger than him. "When do you celebrate your birthday, Janine?"

After looking in the dictionary for the word 'celebrate', Janine gave a little shrug.

"I celebrate my birthday last when I am thirteen years old. No people here feel they can celebrate when we have nothing to eat and no gifts to give each other."

Her eyes filled and she lowered her lashes to hide the tears from George.

"This year, everything is different because the war is over for us. Some of the time, people thought we would never celebrate again," she added sadly.

He was starting to understand just how hard it must have been for them over the last four years of the war. Southern France had been occupied mainly by the Italians and Janine said they were more sympathetic to the French people than the Germans. They shared the same Latin heritage and were just doing what they were told. But most of the food had been taken away to feed enemy troops in other parts of the country, and the French people were left with nothing.

"What did you eat, then? Did you grow vegetables?"

Janine looked over at Mifi.

"My family is large," Mifi replied. "We always grow lots of food in our garden to feed everyone since we were young. For the last four years, everything we grow, we must give to the soldiers. They know exactly what we grow because an Italian officer was living in our house."

She glanced at Janine quickly. There was an uncomfortable silence.

Mifi continued. "We eat snails dug up from the garden. The soldiers did not want that. My mother cooked them very good!"

Janine reached for the dictionary once again. "A neighbor, he had chickens. One time a week, he give children an egg to take home. The soldiers did not know. My brother, Jacquot, he got two because he was so little! We bring the eggs home carefully and my mother make omelet. It is the best meal of every week."

The girls told these stories with a matter-of-fact attitude which showed this had become a way of life, a routine to be endured. George wished he'd brought food to share with them—but of course, it hadn't crossed his mind that they might need it.

Then a thought *did* occur to him. The Americans were hosting a dance the following evening—they always had loads of everything. All the English soldiers had been invited.

George asked Janine if she would come to the dance with him, and explained about the food.

Janine looked excited.

She glanced at Mifi and Michele. Mifi quickly nodded; Michele looked dubious and raised her eyebrows with a questioning look. George wondered why. Then Janine asked for the dictionary.

"Yes, I will like to come to dance. But my mother. She will also come." After finding the word she was looking for, she added with a shy smile, "Chaperone?"

Wow, he'd never heard of that before, but somehow it seemed to go along with what made Janine so special to him.

"Absolutely, yes! I would love to meet her," George said. It was worth a little lie to have Janine give him that smile again.

Janine and brother, Jacquot, 1944

The main square of St. Tropez was lit up with streams of tiny, twinkling lights attached to the trees surrounding the *Place des Lices*. Tables and chairs had been set up. Truckloads of food and drinks had arrived from the harbor. After years of war deprivation, the citizens of St. Tropez were ready for a celebration. Many of the townspeople were sitting and watching the spectacle. The buzz of conversation and greetings added to the carnival atmosphere.

A raised platform served as a stage for the group of American soldiers who had formed a band and were playing lively dance music. The most handsome soldier led the singing. A trumpet wailed. Two trombone players were swinging left to right, perfectly in time to the rhythmic beat of the drummer. Off to the side there was even a piano that had been borrowed from a nearby villa.

So many couples were twirling around, that the sand that served as the dance floor was continuously being kicked up and people appeared to be dancing in a cloud of dust. When the singer began a song called *Boogie Woogie*, the soldiers cheered loudly and demonstrated how the *Jitter Bug* should be danced.

Very soon, the young townspeople were following the lead of their American hosts—boogying, holding a bottle of beer in one hand and their partner in the other. Janine and her mother, Madame Juppet, sat on a bench on the outskirts of the square, in the semi-darkness.

An iconic painting of the dance on
Place des Lices given by the American troops.

Mifi was dancing with a soldier, laughing brightly and being twirled around and around. As they watched, Mifi was offered a taste of beer from the bottle held by her partner.

"Mifi!" Janine's mother called loudly. When Mifi turned around, she made a motion for her to return to the bench. Mifi just waved but did push the bottle away. Madame Juppet sniffed contemptuously.

"The Cerisola family do not have *beacoup de dignité*. It is a shame."

Mifi's family were local, original St. Tropez inhabitants for generations now. There were five children and their upbringing had not been as strict as Janine's. Mifi had been given permission to come to the dance with Janine's mother as her chaperone. That had not counted for much once the music had started and she had been asked to dance by an American soldier.

Janine had been asked to dance as well, but Madame Juppet shook her head no.

Mifi had glanced over at Janine and given her a little smile of sympathy. Then she gave her hand to her soldier and was swept away.

* * *

Janine felt envious but not resentful. She had always been made very aware of her own heritage. The Juppet name could be traced back to thirteenth century aristocracy and was a cause of tremendous pride that would never be lost. More recent family events though, would never be talked about again.

When George had asked her to this celebration she was very excited, yet extremely nervous that her parents would say no. And sure enough, they *had* initially said no. Janine had surprised herself by bursting into tears.

Could she possibly have feelings for this English soldier already?

They had only been together for two short hours, talking in broken French and English. He had seemed so sincere about wanting to know about what had happened during the war. And she just wanted the opportunity to laugh and dance like her friend, Mifi.

George had been on her mind constantly, his strong, tall, athletic body especially. French boys were smaller, and so much...skinnier! George looked so handsome in his uniform. She liked the determined way he walked. The way he had saluted her as if she were a V.I.P.

George Rogers in London shortly after joining Air Sea Rescue in 1942.

It had made her giggle, though, when he started cleaning his toes after walking on the beach. Those big, strong hands wiping away tiny grains of sand before putting on socks. Nobody wore socks here. But she had not liked when his friend made fun of him. No, no, no— nobody should make fun of such a man. George! Even his name was so English, so... solid, somehow.

Through her tears, she had tried to explain to her mother this feeling she had about his honesty. And, of course, she reassured her that she had explained to George about bringing her mother as a chaperone.

"I do not think that dance is appropriate, my dear. All the townspeople will be present. Do you really want to be part of that?"

Oh, yes, Janine would certainly *love* to be part of that.

She was still grateful that her mother had even allowed her to become close with Mifi. It would not have happened but for the war.

It was finally her other good friend, Michele, who had persuaded Madame Juppet to allow her daughter to attend the dance. Michele's opinion was to be trusted. Her father was the town's tax collector and held in high regard by the locals. He also had high ambitions for his only child and she was closely protected—just like Janine.

Janine's heart started beating wildly when she saw another group of men in uniform walking around the periphery of the festivities. They must be English, she thought. Their uniforms were a little different than the ones the American soldiers wore, and they didn't join the raucous laughter and loud cheering coming from the middle of the square.

She focused as hard as she could, but it was difficult to make out faces—beyond the glittering trees everything was in shadow.

This group of soldiers reached the tables laden with food and drinks and started helping themselves. Once their thirst and hunger was satisfied they turned and scanned the crowd, apparently looking for dance partners.

Janine didn't see George among them and heaved a disappointed sigh.

Suddenly she heard a voice by her side. "Bonsoir, Janine. I'm so glad to see you."

The blood rushed to her cheeks and she jumped up to face him. That voice was already so familiar! He was standing alone looking very handsome in his uniform. He put out his large, warm hand to shake hers and it enveloped hers completely. She turned to her mother.

"This is George. I told you we were talking to him and his friends at the beach yesterday."

Madame Juppet gave George a sharp, no-nonsense look and then grudgingly held out her own hand. George shook it enthusiastically and gave her a broad smile.

"Comment allez-vous, madame?"

"Very well, thank you. I am Janine's mother, Madame Juppet. And your full name, young man?"

"George...George Rogers," he replied.

"Please sit down. We will talk."

Janine was so happy to watch George and her mother talking together. He did not appear to be irritated or bored. He had taken the little dictionary from the pocket of his uniform and was doing his best to be understood. Janine's mother, having had a good education, managed quite well to make herself understood in English.

Janine was sad that her own education had suffered because of the war. At one point, her parents felt the need to send her to relatives who lived in the nearby town of Bormes Les Mimosas. They had been very kind, but the only schoolteacher in town had left to fight in the French Resistance.

After a few weeks, she was picked up by her uncle and aunt, Tonton Jacques Dubosc and Tante Germaine. They took her to central France to stay with one of his relatives in a place where she could go back to school.

For reasons that were never explained to Janine, Tonton's relative looked after several young children who were occasionally visited by their parents. Their mothers were local French girls. Their fathers were German soldiers. Janine enjoyed looking after the children, but when she had told her parents about it in a letter, about how the German soldiers would visit, Tonton had come immediately to take her home again.

All that was behind her at last, and Janine tried hard not to think about those times.

After talking together for a few minutes, George asked Madame Juppet for permission to dance with her daughter. To Janine's joy, her mother gave a slight nod and settled herself back on the bench, apparently satisfied.

* * *

The next hour passed in a whirl of dancing and laughter. Mifi was the center of attention when she and her partner danced the swing and she was catapulted through his legs. It was the most daring dance move Janine had ever seen. She looked over at the bench hoping her mother hadn't been looking.

George caught her glance.

"Don't worry, I won't be trying any moves like that. Arm in arm is what I want." Janine gave him a grateful smile as the band played a Glen Miller number. One of the local boys, Phillipe, had once taught her some dance steps and thanks to him, she could now easily follow George's lead.

As they danced past the tables laden with food, Janine's eyes widened. There was probably more food here than she'd seen in a year! George seemed to sense what she was thinking.

"I'm starving. How about you?" he asked.

They cut their dance short and walked over to the food. Janine stared with amazement at the unfamiliar American dishes. There were rolls of bread with what seemed like huge amounts of meat inside. The food servers called them 'ham-*burgers*' and gave her a paper plate with two piled on it. Janine took a bite and then couldn't stop herself—they were delicious! George laughed when she actually asked for a third. Mifi and her dance partner came over and quickly joined the feast.

After that, they were offered sugary pastries with chunks of chocolate inside. The Americans called them 'cook-*ees*'. The girls thought the word 'cook-*ees*' sounded really funny and kept repeating the word until they doubled up with laughter. George loved seeing Janine so relaxed. He couldn't have been happier that she was enjoying their date so much.

He silently blessed the Americans for organizing the event. This celebration of freedom had lifted everyone's spirits.

After hearing the stories of food shortages from the girls, George wasn't surprised to see some of the local people stuffing food into their pockets and handbags— no doubt to share with others who weren't at the dance. The American soldiers helped the cause by good-naturedly packing bags full of cookies to give to their girls. George did the same. As he gave a bag to Janine, she pointed to the other side of the *Place des Lices*.

Madame Juppet was standing up and beckoning. They walked over to the bench together. It was time for them to leave.

"Madame, may I have your permission to see Janine again tomorrow?" George asked apprehensively. Madame Juppet looked over at her daughter's anxious face. After an uneasy pause, she nodded her assent.

"You may come to the house tomorrow evening at five

o'clock for aperitifs. Janine's father will look forward to talking with you." With a big smile on her face, Janine wrote her address on a scrap of paper and gave it to a very happy George.

"See you tomorrow," she said.

"You certainly will!" George replied shaking her hand. He looked at the paper: *Les Marroniers. Avenue Francois Pelletier.*

Didn't seem much of an address.

There wasn't even a number!

And George had no idea what *'aperitifs'* meant.

But what he did know, was that he had passed muster with Madame Juppet. And that meant he would be seeing Janine again.

George stopped in his tracks and took a deep breath. He was standing on the narrow dirt road leading to Janine's home. This was definitely the right place. When he had turned into the road, the blue sign clearly read, *Avenue Francois Pelletier.*

He had seen some nice enough houses on the way but thought he wouldn't be too intimidated by the people who lived in them.

Then he turned the corner.

From where he stood, he could see a pair of enormous iron gates with *Les Marrroniers* cut into the equally impressive stone pillars on either side. He gave a low whistle. What had he got himself into?

Never in his life had he known people who lived in a house like this. He had never even *seen* a house like this.

Janine must be way out of his league. And what was he thinking when he agreed to meet her father?

He considered turning back. Maybe he should have stayed with his friends who were having a drink in town.

* * *

Colin and Basil were at Senequier, a local café. It was one of the only places left intact after the harbor had been bombed by the Germans. The parish church had also been spared during the bombing and its spire could still be seen overlooking the rest of the ruined harbor buildings. George had seen photographs of the harbor as it looked in 1938. Fishing boats tied up on the waterfront and a traditional seafront road with a fish market at one end and the café at the other.

His friends had been boasting about their conquests at the dance. George knew for sure now that most of it was a load of nonsense. If they had got a kiss from one or two of the local girls, they were lucky. The *Place des Lices* had been surrounded by locals and shopkeepers who had stayed open late. They would quickly have reported back any indiscretions to the local families. Even gregarious Mifi had left the dance without a protest when Janine and her mother left. His friends had also teased George mercilessly about his long conversation with the *'old girl'* before he was *'permitted'* to dance with the *'young girl.'* When he told them he was going to Janine's house to meet her family, they roared with laughter.

"Hey, Georgie, you can get anyone you want, for God's sake! Why meet the parents?"

George had been pondering that very question. His unit was only spending ten days docked here. Why waste precious time trying to talk to a girl's parents when he could be scouting the town like his friends? Conversation based on words from a little dictionary would not impress Janine's mother and father. So why...why?

Then Janine's face flashed before his eyes and he knew why.

He'd never met anyone who looked like a movie star before—let alone a French movie star. And there was something about her he just couldn't put into words. George didn't bother telling his friends he was going ahead with his plans. They were so absorbed in drinking and their *'conquests'*, they didn't take much notice when he wandered away.

George had quietly asked directions to *Avenue Francois Pellitier* from the waiter. And he had looked up the meaning of *aperitif* in his dictionary. It made him feel more comfortable that he and the family were just having drinks together. Maybe if he drank enough, things would go smoothly.

George's first view of Janine's home was the 'enormous iron gates with Les Marrroniers cut into impressive stone pillars.'

Now as he stood outside this impressive property, he was wondering if this had been such a good idea.

"George, George. Yes, that's the right house. Ring the bell."

Mifi and Michele had appeared from around the bend in the road and were walking towards him. They gave him a kiss on both cheeks.

"We hope you don't mind that we are here, too. Janine asked if we would come to help make things more fun."

The presence of the girls did make George feel a little less nervous. Well, no turning back now. He was glad the decision had been made for him.

The garden of the villa was filled with bright flowering bushes and graceful palm trees. The two-story house itself was set back inside the property. It was enormous. Wider than four or five adjoining terrace houses together in the East End, he thought. An elaborate stone stairway wound around the outside to the top floor. The ground floor door opened and Janine suddenly appeared on the veranda.

She was wearing a green spotted dress with matching ribbons in her hair. As she ran barefoot across the lawn, her curls bounced with every step. George's eyes went immediately to her shapely tanned legs—gorgeous.

Janine swung back one of the huge gates and beckoned them in. She kissed her friends and offered her cheek to George for the customary double kiss. He obliged with enthusiasm. He loved this wonderful French custom. Her cheeks were soft and she smelled fresh and sweet.

"Bonjour, George. Please come in. My parents are here. You'll meet my father and my brother, Jacquot."

He felt himself sweating. God, he felt so out of place.

"Sure. I've been looking forward to it," he replied with some effort.

Janine led them back across the lawn to the front door. Outside, it had been very hot, humid and extremely bright from the afternoon sun. As soon as they entered the villa, it became cool and almost dark. George had noticed that most houses in these hot countries had thick outer walls, and wooden blinds which were closed during the hottest part of the day. You certainly didn't need that in dreary, rainy old London!

The furniture inside *Les Marroniers* seemed extraordinary to him. Large, extravagantly carved sideboards, tables, chairs—all giving the impression of a family with money. On the walls were oil paintings in ornate wooden frames. God knows what *they* were worth! Glancing down, George could see the floors were covered with tiny mosaic tiles. It made him feel like he was in some kind of a museum.

Janine's parents were waiting in the elaborate dining room where a long, carved wooden table had been laid out with bottles and crystal glasses.

"Entrez, entrez, Mr…?" An elderly-looking man dressed in a suit and tie held out his hand and smiled.

"Rogers. George Rogers. Nice to meet you."

"I am Janine's father, René Juppet. Welcome to our home, George."

George saw a youngster standing at the far end of the room. "And this must be Jacquot. Hello there. Comment ca va?"

Jacquot beamed when he heard his own language being spoken by this stranger. He came and stood by George and blurted out a long reply without taking a breath. This made George smile; kids he understood. There were kids of all ages in his own neighborhood. Jacquot looked about ten years old and was as skinny as a beanpole.

They all sat around the table, he and Janine's dad at one end and the ladies further down. The seats were so big and comfortable that George felt like he was sitting on a throne. Monsieur Juppet poured out a small amount of a yellowish liquid into two sparkling crystal glasses and then filled them to the top with water. He offered one of the glasses to George and settled back comfortably in his chair.

"Cheers!" said George and took a sip. He had no idea what it could be. Hmm, it was pretty good—kind of a licorice flavor. He took a big gulp, but soon noticed that Monsieur Juppet only took small sips. He followed suit. The ladies weren't drinking the yellow alcohol, but had filled their own glasses with red wine. George was surprised to see that Jacquot was given wine and water mixed. Kind of young for wine, he thought. He'd have to ask Janine about that.

"So, George, tell me about yourself, please. Where were you born?"

Monsieur Juppet spoke English well and George figured he wouldn't need the dictionary. Thank God for *that*, at least. In these intimidating surroundings, George felt the need to exaggerate a bit about his life before the war. He didn't want to have to translate those embellishments as well!

"Have you ever been to London?" he started.

"No, I have not had that pleasure, George."

Perfect. Now he could lay it on a bit.

"My family live in the East End of London. We live in a house by the River Thames. My father works as a carpenter and my mother looks after the family and the household. I've got an older brother and two younger sisters. Aunts, uncles, and cousins, live and work nearby."

So far, that was true, the part about his family anyway. The Rogers actually lived in a tiny flat, not a house.

*George, older brother James, and younger sister Sylvia,
in front of their block of flats in Shoreditch, East London.
George is approximately seven years old.*

"I was eighteen and had just finished school when I joined up in '42. I loved school, did very well. Always first in class," George boasted, knowing he had to make a good impression if he wanted to see Janine again.

He took another small sip from his glass. The truth was, George *did* like school, and *had* done very well.

What he didn't tell Monsieur Juppet was that his family were dirt poor. He left school at fourteen to help with the family finances, and had to take accounting classes in the evenings because he was working full-time. When he headed back to London in a few months, there might not even be a home! The East End had been bombed to smithereens, including their tiny flat.

Monsieur Juppet took George's empty glass and filled it again. George took the opportunity to turn the conversation back to St. Tropez.

"Janine has told me a little about what it was like in St. Tropez during the occupation. It must have been hard for the whole family."

St. Tropez harbor after the final bombing by the Germans at the very end of the war.

"The Nazis, they were very cruel," said Monsieur Juppet heatedly. "When they knew they were losing the war, the Italians withdrew from the south of France and went back home. The Nazis sent airplanes here and bombed our beautiful town. The harbor was bombed and a bomb was dropped on the *Places des Lices*. The square was being used as a hospital and had a large white cloth with a red cross hanging over the trees. It did not matter. There were many casualties. I will never forget that day."

George was shocked and fascinated with hearing this first-hand account of life in an occupied country. He also felt more comfortable after the third drink that Monsieur Juppet called pastis. He would ask for that next time he went to a bar with his friends.

All this while, Jacquot sat by their side staring with fascination at George's uniform. He didn't understand what they were saying, but when there was a pause, he pointed to George's insignia.

"What is this?" Jacquot asked.

'It shows I'm in the Air Force. Specifically, the Air Sea Rescue."

Monsieur Juppet translated that for Jacquot and George let him try on his uniform cap. Jacquot, like any young boy, started pretending to shoot down the enemy, and his father told George that he thanked God that his son would never be in a war. He himself had been badly wounded during the First World War and had been honorably discharged. At least he had been home this time to try to look after his family.

The three girls and Janine's mother were chattering at the other end of the table and occasionally glancing in their direction. The men talked together for almost an hour and then Monsieur Juppet got up and held out his hand.

"Au revoir, George. It was good getting to know you and *about* you. Most interesting. You may see my daughter again if she wishes. Her mother and I approve."

Then he held out his arm to Madame Juppet and they turned and left the room.

Janine's father and mother, Rene and Charlotte Juppet, with Janine and brother Jacques, standing in front of Les Marroniers, showing off their new car. 1945.

"**G**ermaine, would it be OK if Janine took me to visit the Chapelle Sainte-Anne after lunch?" George asked Janine's aunt who was visiting from Marseilles where she lived with her husband, Jacques. "She told me there is a good view of St. Tropez up there. We could both do with a nice, long walk after that delicious dandelion omelet."

George had never imagined he'd ever eat a meal of weeds that grew between the concrete slabs that made up his backyard at home in London. He'd eaten some pretty nasty things in his time. Eels in liquor had been pretty disgusting. His mum served them up at least once a week, but you ate what you were given. When Janine had asked him to pick dandelions with her for lunch, he'd laughed out loud, thinking she was joking.

"Oh, they are good, George. I think you will like them."

He and Janine had been allowed to take the short walk to the neighbor's house for some fresh eggs and gathered the dandelion leaves on the way back. Yep, it really had been delicious! Maybe he'd ask Madame Juppet for the recipe to give to his mum. The thought made him smile. He'd be home soon, back to egg and chips and roly poly. Thinking of pudding and custard made his mouth water.

"Oh, yes!" Germaine started rolling up her embroidered napkin and put it carefully in the silver-plated napkin holder. "That is a very good idea. As Charlotte and René have already gone to take their sieste, I am happy to walk with you. Just give me a few minutes to digest my food and I'll be ready to go."

George's heart sank, but he didn't let it show. Was this really the way it would be for the rest of this week? There was only four days left before they were due to ship out from St. Tropez for good.

* * *

Over the last few days, he and Janine had been alone for short periods of time, but never out of sight of a relative or close neighbor. His unit was heading to the city of Toulon next to help the citizens there clean up and readjust to their pre-war lives. So, should he just give up?

Tante Germaine sitting on Rene's lap. Jacquot and Charlotte on Tonton Jacque's lap. Janine, Michele and Mifi. George and Janine were hardly ever out of sight of a relative or close neighbor.

Especially now that Germaine was in the picture, too.

Tante Germaine and her husband had no children and she obviously adored Janine and Jacquot. She had spent the last few days accompanying her niece whenever she was on a *'date'* with George. He didn't understand if this was still part of the chaperoning custom round here, or if she just enjoyed their company. Janine never questioned her aunt about it and was always calm and polite. On top of that, Jacquot often tagged along as well, chatting and running alongside like an eager puppy. Sometimes Jacquot would see some of his young friends and then it became a circus.

Yesterday, there had been ten of them playing boules on the *Place des Lices*.

When they had first arrived at the square mid-morning, there had been some stalls set up selling fruit and vegetables. This had been an age-old custom in all small towns before the war, but then the occupying soldiers had taken everything they could find to feed themselves. Now peaches, tomatoes, and peppers were being sold again, and often bartered for other items. Money was still in short supply. Albert and Mifi were there and had sold all the vegetables that their father had sent with them. Now they could have some fun.

Janine, George, Jacquot and one of his friends made up one team. Mifi, Michele, and two more friends, made up the other. Germaine sat on one of the benches at the side chatting with some of the local women.

The whole square was filled with people playing this French version of bowling. There were no bowling lanes, though, and as he watched, George was amazed people didn't get hurt. One team's player would start by throwing out a small wooden ball called a cochonnet.

George looked this up in his dictionary and was surprised to see it translated literally to *piglet*. Janine didn't know quite why but told him it was also called *le but* which meant target or goal. That name made more sense to George because the object of the game was to roll your larger ball as close to it as possible. It got dangerous when they'd throw the heavy metal balls high in the air to try and smash their opponents' ball out of the way. Sometimes the balls that were hit would ricochet in all directions. The men took it very seriously, and would measure carefully after each round using pieces of straw. The winner might be only an eighth of an inch nearer to the target ball which then, of course, led to heated discussions.

George had a great idea.

"Janine, please show me how to hold the ball properly." Janine smiled, quickly took his hand and placed his fingers in the right position. That simple contact confirmed the intense feelings they felt for each other and George knew he'd have to find a way to be alone with her before too long.

Playing boules had been lots of fun. The players on both teams had been greatly amused watching George try out this game. On one of his first throws, his ball had hit a tree, rebounded, and landed with a heavy thud on a man's foot. The man just happened to be Mifi's older brother, Albert, who was supposed to be keeping an eye on her. In pain, he hopped off home and Mifi was again free of a chaperone. George couldn't help laughing along with the crowd of local people who had gathered round to cheer the awkward English player on.

He heartily embraced the warmth these people obviously felt for him, and it made him feel welcome into their tight-knit community. They appreciated that George was always trying to speak French to them, using his dictionary less and less as he became more proficient.

* * *

On the way back to *Les Marroniers* after the game, Germaine and Janine told George more about their family and the house. George asked Germaine if she had lived there when she was young.

"But no, St. Tropez is not my home. It is not my sister's home. Our maiden name was Martel, a very old, well-known family in Lyon. The Juppet family is originally from Alsace-Lorraine. That was many centuries ago, and many of the Juppet family now live in central France. Our heritage is impeccable, yes, impeccable."

"Why did you move to St. Tropez?" George inquired. "Was it to do with the war?"

"No, it was not the war, George. If only that were so. I will tell you our story as I can see you are very *sympatique*."

Germaine took a deep breath.

"My husband and Janine's father owned a leather goods and woodworking factory in Nice until Janine was ten years old. It was bought for them by my grandfather. He had a lot of money and wanted his granddaughters to benefit from it. Buying a business for his son-in-laws seemed a perfect way to do it. It was wonderful for a while. Ah, we had money, beautiful clothes, afternoon strolls along the promenade, and then evenings spent dancing with friends. We thought it would be like this forever."

Germaine seemed to enjoy reminiscing about her life of just a few years ago as she stared ahead dreamily. Then her voice changed.

"But René and Jacques, they were not good businessmen. They trusted people. They are good people, and they think everyone is like them. We learned that is not so."

The leather goods and woodworking factory in Nice.

Germaine gave Janine a sidelong glance.

"We lost everything to wicked people who tricked our husbands. One day, our home, the factory—they were all gone. Jacques and I got help from his family and we bought a little house in Marseilles. René was too proud to ask the Juppet or Martel families for a house or money."

George turned to look at Janine. Tears had filled her eyes. She was weeping softly.

"You don't have to tell me anymore. I think I understand."

"It is all right, George," said Janine. "I want you to know my life. It has been a lovely life, but sometimes it was difficult, too."

"Yes, I can see it must have been really hard on you. Changing towns, school, friends…I get it. And then the war comes. Did you feel safe in your home?"

"Yes, we did feel safe at first. But then Madame Bertier was asked to take in an Italian officer. It was not good after that."

"Who's Madame Bertier?"

"*Les Marroniers* is her house. She lives upstairs. She is very old and does not go out. Madame Bertier told the Italian officer that he had to stay downstairs with us. She was too old to cook and clean for him."

George was astonished to learn that the Juppet family did not own *Les Marroniers*. Madame Bertier lived upstairs, and they rented the downstairs from her. Most of those beautiful paintings and furnishings didn't even belong to them. That proud, aristocratic family did not own any home. When they had sold their house in Nice to pay off the many debts they owed after the business went bankrupt, René had decided they must move away from Nice, and look for somewhere in a small town. It was too expensive to live in a big city. So that is why they now lived in St. Tropez. It was a pleasant town, but it did not have the life and culture of Nice.

René had eventually found a job as a draftsman in the local torpedo factory. Before that, they had to regularly barter the family's inherited valuables in exchange for food, clothing and other essentials.

"My father was very unhappy for a long time," Janine said sadly. "He would spend many days in his bedroom and we would not see him. Then a friend from Nice found him the job at the torpedo factory, and he is now a man again. My mother is happy that we still have some of our family heirlooms left. That is important to her. I do not care. I want us to be a happy family again."

George felt very sorry hearing these stories about the Juppet family but, on the other hand, it made him feel more comfortable knowing that Janine was also the daughter of a poor family.

Maybe she wasn't way out of his league, after all.

Still, he didn't want to think about her meeting his own family and where he lived. Oh no! That would be completely out of the question.

He deliberately started talking about the game of boules they had just played, and they were soon laughing again. That's what was needed—lots of laughs. The sad family history of the Rogers of Shoreditch should wait.

It was Mifi who had told George about the Chapelle Saint-Anne. She said it was an ancient chapel built to thank Saint Anne for saving the inhabitants of St. Tropez from the plague in the seventeenth century.

Mifi was obviously proud of her town's history, but she was also very practical and somewhat devious.

The chapel was built on the very top of a hill overlooking her town, and Mifi had hinted that the long, uphill walk might tire out Germaine.

Better still, Mifi had advised George that he should suggest walking there after lunch and having her sieste might win out over Germaine joining them.

After all, George had never expressed his impatience with this constant supervision and may possibly be allowed some time alone with Janine.

Michele had also been there when this plan was made, and the three friends had giggled like the schoolgirls they were.

Well, it hadn't quite worked out the way George had hoped, so now Plan B was in operation.

Germaine, Janine and George set off from *Les Marroniers* at a quick pace and, sure enough by the time they were halfway there, Germaine had fallen behind. It was the middle of the day, and the temperature was in the high eighties. Luckily, it was that time of year when the mistral—the strong wind that blows through southern France—was in full force and the wind made the climb easier. Even though George was brought up in England, a country where it was cool most of the time, he was oblivious to the heat. Being with Janine alone was all he could think about.

She looked adorable and he needed to tell her that.

The mountain was covered with pine trees. Janine picked up a pine cone and showed George the pine nuts imbedded deep inside the cones. She explained that this had been another source of nourishment during the war.

"Mifi, Michelle, and I used to spend hours collecting the nuts, and then smashing each shell with heavy stones to get the tiny nuts out. We were so proud when we could at last bring them home to our mothers."

George had never tasted them before and they enjoyed hunting for the delicious nuts on the way up.

Before they knew it, they had almost reached the top. They paused for breath and took in the view. Looking down from this vantage point, the damage from the recent bombing was completely hidden.

The distinctive red ochre rooftops of the houses stood out among swaying trees and rose-colored laurel bushes. In the distance, reflections of the sun shimmered over the vividly blue sea. The view brought to mind a painting George had seen on his recent travels.

They gazed down–in awe of the beauty.

Finally, George held out his hand to her and they continued climbing together. After a short while, George stopped, turned to Janine, and reached for her other hand.

"I'm going to miss seeing you when we ship out on Sunday. Maybe we can write to each other?"

George and Janine gazed down—in awe of the beauty.

"Oh, George, I will miss you, too. It is hard, so hard, for me to believe our first meeting was only a few days ago at *Les Graniers.*"

George knew he would never forget that meeting. The moment he realized the girl on the beach was unlike any other he had ever met.

He looked down the hill. Germaine had sat down on a large rock and was looking away from them, back down the rocky path.

Was she deliberately giving them some time to be alone?

George pulled Janine towards him and drew her quickly between the laurel bushes that lined the path.

"I will never forget our first meeting, Janine. I've

thought about you every minute since. When you didn't show up the next day, I was sure you weren't interested in me."

Janine stared up into his eyes. Lifting herself on tiptoes, she kissed him shyly on the lips. He gently held her close and passionately returned the kiss. He had never waited so long to kiss a girl and it was hard to hold back.

It was obvious to him that Janine was inexperienced, but her ardor pushed all propriety out of George's mind. He moved further off the path and Janine followed willingly, caressing George's neck and shoulders. They were soon kissing deeply and desperately.

It felt as though time stood still.

"Janine, George, where are you? Come back here at once!" Germaine's voice got louder and more strident. "Janine, now! Come here quickly!"

Germaine's loud shouts made Janine jump and she opened her eyes in panic. She looked around as if she'd just woken up from a deep dream. George let her go and caressed her cheek softly.

"I'm sorry. I should never have done that. Please forgive me."

Janine looked at him and her glance seemed questioning.

Was she questioning him or herself?

George quickly adjusted his uniform while Janine straightened the collar of her dress. Then, she turned and ran quickly back to the path.

George followed, picking up Janine's scarf that had fallen from her shoulders. He ran his fingers over the soft material and quickly put it into one of the pockets of his uniform.

Chapelle Saint-Anne.

Germaine was now up ahead of them on the path leading to the chapel. She gave them both a sharp look when first Janine, and then George, reappeared. There was no hint of a smile and she shook her head in dismay.

"Sorry, Tante Germaine, George saw a beautiful flower he wanted to pick for me just off the path and I was holding back the branches for him."

George was impressed that Janine had quickly come up with a story that sounded so convincing. Or so he thought.

"So, where is this flower?" demanded Germaine.

Oh, boy.

"Well, then I thought better of it, Madame Dubosc. I remembered my mum always says to leave nature alone."

George imagined she would appreciate this kind of reason, and it made him smile inwardly to imagine his Cockney London mother saying that. His poor mum had probably never seen nature of any kind in her life.

"Come, we must return now. We have been away too long and my sister will be worried."

Germaine made an imperious gesture prompting Janine to walk in front. Janine did what she was told without a word.

George spent the downward climb trying to chat innocently to Germaine about the history of the Chapelle Saint-Anne.

He hoped that one day he would be able to return and climb to the top.

Germaine was not responsive.

George wondered if he would be allowed to see Janine again.

* * *

George had not seen or heard from Janine for two days. His unit was due to leave St. Tropez the next day, and he knew he could not go without saying goodbye.

He blamed himself for not setting up another date after their very awkward descent from Chapelle Saint-Anne.

When they had arrived back at *Les Marroniers*, Germaine had unlocked the gates and motioned for Janine to go in ahead of her.

Germaine had then said au revoir to George and closed the gates firmly behind her. He had watched Janine walk despondently through the garden, but she had turned around before entering the house and given a little wave.

"Au revoir, Janine, au revoir," he had called.

Lying in his bunk, he had been practicing his French again, and noticed something interesting. In his little dictionary, *—au revoir* was also translated as *—see you again.* He had called *au revoir* to Janine and that was what he intended to do. George sat up, his thoughts and emotions suddenly uplifted.

He would ask Janine's friends for help.

Michele spoke better English, but her house was as much a fortress as Janine's. So, he would go to Mifi.

George jumped up and went to ask the officer-in-charge for a half-day leave.

"Given!" said the officer. "But be back by 1800 hours. Departure is 0800 hours tomorrow."

George was easily able to find his way to Mifi's home, *Lou Paradou*. He remembered seeing it at the beginning of *Avenue Francois Pelletier*. As he approached the house, he heard loud shouting, laughter, and a woman's voice calling out.

"Assez! Assez! Enough! It is lunchtime. Come in. Now!"

George ran up to the fence just in time to catch Albert finishing up a game of croquet they had been playing in the garden. He caught Albert's attention and asked if he could speak to Mifi.

"Certainly, George. But come in and have lunch with us first. My parents will be happy to see you!"

The Cerisolas were a cheerful, hard-working family, always welcoming people with open arms. A cheer went up when he entered the small dining room, and everyone moved over to make room for the unexpected guest.

The table was laden.

In addition to the food they sold at the market, Monsieur Cerisola and the boys worked hard growing enough fruit and vegetables to keep themselves well-fed.

Madame Cerisola brought over a huge tureen and placed it in the middle of the wooden table. Mifi brought over bread, grated cheese and a bowl of milk. She then sat down next to George. Vegetable soup, with a sweet-smelling bouquet was placed in bowls and passed around the table. The bread, cheese, and milk followed.

George helped himself liberally, and took his first taste. It was probably the most delicious food he had ever tasted in his life. He looked over at Madame Cerisola with a smile and she gave a satisfied nod.

Jacquot, Mifi, Janine, Michele and Albert,
sometime around 1944.

After lunch, the children went outside again, while their parents and grandmother took their sieste.

Mifi told George they should wait until four o'clock to try and see Janine, as the Juppet family would not like to be interrupted during this traditionally quiet time of day.

George accepted that she was right, but every minute counted now—and how did he know that Janine was even there today? He went outside and tried to join in the game of croquet the children had resumed, but he couldn't relax. He paced up and down waiting for the deadline.

When it was time, Mifi took him along the outer fence that ran alongside *Les Marroniers* and stopped outside one of the shuttered windows. She bent down and picked up some gravel from the roadway, and threw a handful as hard as she could through the fence. Some pieces hit the shutters.

Almost immediately, the shutters opened and Janine leaned out. When she saw George, her face lit up with that film star smile that he had been thinking about since he had last seen her.

Did it mean she still liked him?

Had she forgiven him for his pushing himself on her?

His heart missed a beat.

God, could you fall in love so quickly?

"One minute," Janine whispered. "I will let you in."

He and Mifi waited by the gates and Janine came running across the garden. She swung open the gate and came to a halt in front of George. He took her hand gently and kissed it.

Suddenly, her father's voice rang out.

"Bonjour, Mifi. Bonjour Monsieur, Rogers. Welcome. Please come in."

George swallowed hard and followed Janine and Mifi to the door.

"An aperitif?" asked Monsieur Juppet.

"Yes, of course! I would love to join you," replied George.

They entered the dim, cool house and Monsieur Juppet hurriedly opened the china cabinet to take out two glasses. He then opened the enormous wooden armoire and took out the pastis. As he was pouring it out, Madame Juppet appeared at the dining room door doing up the last of the buttons on her blouse. They had obviously been abruptly woken from their afternoon rest. She gave George a serious stare, then sat down at the table near Janine and Mifi.

George told Monsieur Juppet that his unit was on the way to Toulon the following day. Mentioning Toulon prompted Monsieur Juppet to share a story about the family visiting the city before the war. He reminisced about the beauty of its fountains in the many small squares. He hoped they had not been damaged when Toulon had been bombed.

George listened as patiently as he could, but couldn't help looking down at his watch. Monsieur Juppet was taking his time describing one particular fountain in agonizing detail. Monsieur Juppet caught the glance and asked George if he was in a hurry to go somewhere.

"Monsieur Juppet, my unit is leaving very early tomorrow morning and I must be back on board today by 1800 hours. Please…may I take Janine for a walk to the port so we can say goodbye? You are welcome to come. Mifi, too."

"Yes, of course you may, George. Now I understand your urgency. You should have interrupted me earlier. You are very polite. Madame Juppet and I were talking about that a few days ago. Is that not so, Charlotte?"

"Yes, René," replied his wife, but her tone seemed cold and detached.

Her husband raised his eyebrows in surprise, but said nothing. Madame Juppet got up quickly and started clearing the table. George figured that Germaine had told her sister what had happened on their walk to the chapel, but had not shared it with Janine's father. Thank God for that!

"I will also come. Germaine is away visiting a friend," said Madame Juppet. "Come, Janine, let us get something warm to put on our shoulders. The mistral is blowing again today."

The harbor at St. Tropez.

The walk to the harbor was punctuated by uncomfortable silences. George tried his hardest to engage Madame Juppet in conversation, but at most he received one or two word replies. As they neared the waterfront, Mifi took control.

"Madame Juppet, George told me you made him a delicious dandelion omelet. I am very envious of your cooking skills. Tell me, what is the secret?"

Janine smiled at her friend's craftiness. Madame Juppet

could never resist holding forth on her many methods of cooking this simple egg dish. George offered Janine his arm and they took the opportunity to walk on ahead in relative privacy.

Janine gestured at the bombed-out buildings along the harbor front.

"Oh, George. Not long ago, it was crowded here each day. It was a place for everyone to sit, and talk over a glass of lemonade or cup of expresso. I would meet my friends and we would spend fun times together. We would try not to think about war all the time."

George's mind went back to the picture he had seen, what it had looked like before the bombing, before the citizens of St. Tropez had endured the devastating destruction of their harbor and fishing boats. Janine told him the town vowed to rebuild the harbor so it would look exactly like it had before the war.

Janine's hand was resting on George's arm and he gently covered it with his own hand.

"Janine, I want to say sorry. I am sorry for my coarse behavior on the road up to the Chapelle Saint-Anne. You are so beautiful and mean so much to me, but I could not stop myself. Tell me, do you forgive me?"

Janine patted George's hand meaningfully and then let her hand rest on his.

"Forgive? Why do I need to forgive you? We both feel passion. It could not be helped."

She smiled at the recollection.

"Tante Germaine was shocked, that is true. She told my mother we had kissed…I think she just wanted to protect me."

"What do you mean, protect you? I would never—"

"George, I have not told you why my parents sent me to live with Tonton's relatives during the war. I think you should know."

George stared at her, not quite understanding. It seemed simple enough. She had stayed with relatives during part of the war. So what? But now he was intrigued.

"I do want to know everything about you, Janine. So please, tell me."

Janine swallowed hard and lowered her lashes over her eyes. She spoke in hushed tones.

"Germaine told you there was an Italian officer stationed at *Les Marroniers* during the war. When he first came, I was fourteen years old, and I thought he was a gentleman. My father was an officer, and he had always told me that officers were gentlemen. But this one was *not*."

Janine looked up at George with tears in her eyes.

"Once, I woke up during the night and he was standing at my door staring down at me. When he saw my eyes were open, he smiled. Then he shut the door quietly and went back to his room. I thought he might have gone to the wrong bedroom by mistake and I said nothing.

"Then I would see him sitting on the bed in his room. He kept the door a little open and would stare at me as I passed by. It made me feel very uncomfortable. Was it my fault? Was I doing something wrong to make him look at me like that? I did not tell my parents. What could they do? I did not want them to get in trouble with our enemy.

"Then, one night, I was awake and heard my bedroom door open and he came in. George, he smiled at me. This terrible man smiled at me! I was so scared. At first, I couldn't speak. I could not even breathe. Suddenly, he started walking over to my bed. I will never forget the look on his face. I knew this time it was not a mistake. I took a deep breath and found my voice.

"Then I screamed! He quickly turned to leave, but my parents saw him entering his own room again. I told them what had happened. It was terrible for them, because they knew they could not accuse this enemy of any impropriety.

"They would be locked away and then he would have his way. So, the very next day, my Tonton took me to stay with relatives. I could not be here with my own family and friends."

"Janine, my darling, Janine!" George didn't know what to say. He wanted to hold her and never let her go.

"I have not finished my story yet, George. There is more." Her voice was trembling so much that he had to lean in close to hear her.

"A few weeks ago, one of our good friends, someone Mifi and I went to school with, was accused of collaborating with the enemy. That is what they called it when a girl was known to have been friends with one of our enemies. She was accused of having a child with *that* officer—that very same terrible man who lived in our home."

She paused.

"George, these people from my town took her to the *Place des Lices* and shaved off all her hair. Everyone was watching, everyone was calling her horrible, horrible names. She has left St. Tropez and can never come back."

Janine paused again and whispered.

"Since I saw that happening, I have terrible dreams. In

my dreams the girl is *me*. It is me everyone is calling names. I can feel the razor taking off *my* hair. I was afraid to go to sleep."

Janine looked into George's eyes. More tears welled up.

Il n'y a pas de coïncidence...there are no coincidences.

George's brief entry into her life had been for a reason. Of this, she was now certain. And she wanted to explain that to him.

"Until I met you on the beach, I had not trusted anyone. I could not let any boy—not one—even touch me. But...you...you, George, have made me feel well again. That is what I want to tell you before you go. Thank you. I am better because of you and I will never forget you for that. And I will never forget your voice, your eyes, your hands, your...patience and honesty."

George knew he would never forget Janine either.

Whatever happened in the future, he would always remember the time he had spent with her.

The look they exchanged was filled with love and longing.

"Monsieur Rogers. It is time for you to get back to your ship. It is nearly six o'clock." Madame Juppet was now standing behind them. "Say goodbye quickly. We must go back also. It is nearly dinnertime."

They crossed the harbor road together in silence.

A small boat was waiting by the dock to take soldiers to the ships anchored off shore. The last stragglers were boarding.

Albert and Michelle were also waiting there to say goodbye. George shook hands with Madame Juppet and gave the traditional kiss on each cheek to the friends.

When he came to Janine, he hugged her closely and kissed each cheek tenderly.

"And I will remember you always, my darling," he whispered in her ear.

Then he had to let her go.

He turned quickly and went on board without looking back.

Acknowledgments

My deepest thanks go to my daughters, Janine Manley and Mary Battaglia, for their love of family. That was the inspiration for this story. Mary also helped tremendously by giving me immediate feedback whenever I needed encouragement and advice during the writing process.

Thanks to my dear sister, Christine Fleming, who provided many photographs and whose memory for details makes this story more authentic.

Lastly, sincere thanks to my editor and now friend, Richard Kelley, who kept me on track time after time, and Francine DAlessandro whose memoir writing workshop put me on this track some two years ago.

About the Author

Elizabeth Battaglia was born and raised in London, England. She came to the U.S after meeting her American husband, Vince, and now lives in the Hudson Valley, New York.

Her two loving daughters, Janine and Mary, and two wonderful grandchildren live nearby.

After a rewarding career in education, Elizabeth began writing and capturing all the family stories she had collected over the years. She is now so happy to be able to share the first of these stories with her extended family and beyond.

*With thanks to Wikipedia Commons
and the respective picture authors:*

Page 8 (St. Tropez) *Ryodo477*
Page 59 (Chapelle Saint-Anne) *Starus*
Page 65 (St. Tropez Harbor) *Adrian77*

Made in the USA
San Bernardino, CA
19 June 2017